365 Affirmations to Absolutely Guarantee a Record-Breaking Year

John Di Lemme

D1292206

365 Affirmations to Absolutely Guarantee a Record-Breaking Year © 2012 John Di Lemme

Di Lemme Development Group, Inc.
931 Village Boulevard
Suite 905-366
West Palm Beach, Florida 33409-1939
877-277-3339
www.LifestyleFreedomClub.com

About the Author

In September 2001, John Di Lemme founded Di Lemme Development Group, Inc., a company known worldwide for its role in expanding the personal development industry. As president and CEO, John strives for excellence in every area of his business and believes that you must surround yourself with a like-minded team in order to stay on top of your game.

In addition to building a successful company, John has changed lives around the globe as an international motivational speaker. Over the past ten years, he has shared the stage with the best of the best including Dr. John Maxwell, Dennis Waitley, Jim Rohn, Les Brown, and Rich Devos only to name a few. John was also featured on Zig Ziglar's webcast. This is truly an amazing feat for someone that was clinically diagnosed as a stutterer at a very young age and told that he would never speak fluently.

John truly believes that everyone needs personal development to reach their full potential in life, and his determination to reach all forms of media with his motivational messages has catapulted his career. John has produced over two hundred fifty products and is an accomplished author of eleven books including his latest bestselling book, "7 Principles to Live a Champion Life."

John has also been featured on national and international television and radio programs throughout the world. As a multi-million dollar entrepreneur, John is one of the most highly sought after strategic business coaches in the world.

John's passion is to teach others how to live a champion life despite the label that society has placed on them. Through his books, audio/video materials, sold-out live seminars, intensive training boot camps, live webinars, Closing & Marketing University, and Lifestyle Freedom Club memberships, John has made success a reality for thousands worldwide.

Grab a Hold of John's FREE Video... 1
The Top *11* Motivational Quotes to Overcome Fear
& Ultimately Earn Millions at www.177Quotes.com

Affirmation #1

I am committed to do whatever it takes for as long as it takes to be a Why Warrior 1000%.

Affirmation #2

I am a Faithful Dreamer!

Affirmation #3

I am living in the Kingdom of Freedom with Massive Monumental Miracle Expectation.

Affirmation #4

I am confidently walking strong as a Faithful Why Warrior Champion.

Grab a Hold of John's FREE Video...   2
The Top *11* Motivational Quotes to Overcome Fear
& Ultimately Earn Millions at www.177Quotes.com

Affirmation #5

I am getting Healthier by the second.

Affirmation #6

I am driving Indecision right out of my life NOW!

Affirmation #7

I am believing for a Miracle.

Affirmation #8

I am ripping the negative label off of me right NOW!

Grab a Hold of John's FREE Video...   3
The Top *11* Motivational Quotes to Overcome Fear
& Ultimately Earn Millions at www.177Quotes.com

Affirmation #9

I am an Abundant Giver of encouragement to everyone that I see.

Affirmation #10

My Dream loves me; that's why I am a Champion.

Affirmation #11

I am opening today's present with Explosive Focused Expectation for a Supernatural Miracle.

Affirmation #12

I am driving my Faith by my Words Now!

Grab a Hold of John's FREE Video...   4
The Top *11* Motivational Quotes to Overcome Fear
& Ultimately Earn Millions at www.177Quotes.com

Affirmation #13

I am determined to increase my focus
second by second.

Affirmation #14

I am building my strength!

Affirmation #15

I am stepping into enemy territory with
faith to defeat the enemy of
procrastination.

Affirmation #16

I am a persistent and prosperous life-
changing Champion.

Grab a Hold of John's FREE Video... 5
The Top *11* Motivational Quotes to Overcome Fear
& Ultimately Earn Millions at www.177Quotes.com

Affirmation #17

I am releasing ALL negative thoughts out
of my heart & mind Now!

Affirmation #18

Greater is the Why that is in me than the
fear that is trying to steal my destiny.

Affirmation #19

I am speaking affirmations out loud all
day to build my faith.

Affirmation #20

Nothing is impossible for me, because I
am a Why Warrior Laser-Focused
Champion!

Grab a Hold of John's FREE Video...   6
The Top *11* Motivational Quotes to Overcome Fear
& Ultimately Earn Millions at www.177Quotes.com

Affirmation #21

My mindset is set in rock solid cement.

Affirmation #22

I will not be moved from my Why Warrior
Success Journey!

Affirmation #23

My focused determination predicts
my Why.

Affirmation #24

I am achieving Lifestyle Freedom Today!

Grab a Hold of John's FREE Video... 7
The Top *11* Motivational Quotes to Overcome Fear
& Ultimately Earn Millions at www.177Quotes.com

Affirmation #25

I am a Mentor to millions worldwide.

Affirmation #26

I am pulverizing the enemy of fear now with my outwardly spoken words.

Affirmation #27

I am achieving my Why!

Affirmation #28

I am taking full responsibility today for the achievement and advancement of my Why in life.

Grab a Hold of John's FREE Video... 8
The Top *11* Motivational Quotes to Overcome Fear
& Ultimately Earn Millions at www.177Quotes.com

Affirmation #29

I am a unique miracle created by God to live out God's purpose for me right NOW!

Affirmation #30

Fear trembles at the sound of my voice, because my words demolish fear INSTANTLY!

Affirmation #31

My words are brilliantly orchestrated in creating miracles in my life now

Grab a Hold of John's FREE Video... 9
The Top *11* Motivational Quotes to Overcome Fear
& Ultimately Earn Millions at www.177Quotes.com

Affirmation #32

I am building a fortress around my Heart to defend it against the works of the enemy.

Affirmation #33

I am responsible for the direction of my life!

Affirmation #34

I love challenging myself second by second.

Affirmation #35

I am a Faith Fighter for my Why!

Grab a Hold of John's FREE Video... 10
The Top *11* Motivational Quotes to Overcome Fear
& Ultimately Earn Millions at www.177Quotes.com

Affirmation #36

I am taking the enemy of fear captive now by my outward spoken faith-filled Champion words.

Affirmation #37

I am an Extraordinary Winner!

Affirmation #38

I am a strong, wiser, powerful, decisive, miracle manifesting, Champion Why Warrior!

Affirmation #39

I am shocking my bank teller today!

Grab a Hold of John's FREE Video... 11
The Top *11* Motivational Quotes to Overcome Fear
& Ultimately Earn Millions at www.177Quotes.com

Affirmation #40

Enough is enough! The Success Overflow
has begun in my life Now!

Affirmation #41

I am resisting default!

Affirmation #42

I am a Supernatural Sower that will reap
a Supernatural Harvest!

Affirmation #43
I am exchanging my negative friends for
encouraging, empowering, fired-up
Champions.

Grab a Hold of John's FREE Video... 12
The Top *11* Motivational Quotes to Overcome Fear
& Ultimately Earn Millions at www.177Quotes.com

Affirmation #44

My Why is absolutely crystal clear.

Affirmation #45

My personal economy is explosive, because I've planted the right seeds.

Affirmation #46

I am a seed of supernatural greatness that God has planted on Earth for a massive miracle.

Affirmation #47

I'm loving the success process, because I am a Champion Eagle.

Grab a Hold of John's FREE Video... 13
The Top *11* Motivational Quotes to Overcome Fear
& Ultimately Earn Millions at www.177Quotes.com

Affirmation #48

I am challenging myself each day to manifest the blessed life that I have a right to live.

Affirmation #49

Success is a cinch for me, because I was born a Champion!

Affirmation #50

My prosperity is solely based on one fact and one fact only...I am a Champion!

Affirmation #51

I am increasing my learning daily to achieve my Why NOW!

Grab a Hold of John's FREE Video... 14
The Top *11* Motivational Quotes to Overcome Fear
& Ultimately Earn Millions at www.177Quotes.com

Affirmation #52

I have a right to live Lifestyle Freedom!

Affirmation #53

I am a shining example of a Champion
with honor & integrity.

Affirmation #54

My construction zone represents
my miracle.

Affirmation #55

I am willing to pay the price for success!

Grab a Hold of John's FREE Video...   15
The Top *11* Motivational Quotes to Overcome Fear
& Ultimately Earn Millions at www.177Quotes.com

Affirmation #56

I am walking tall, standing strong and
expecting a miracle.

Affirmation #57

I am living a remarkable, wonderful,
breathtaking life!

Affirmation #58

My words are terminating fear out of
my life NOW!

Affirmation #59

I am challenging myself every day to get
to the next level.

Grab a Hold of John's FREE Video... 16
The Top *11* Motivational Quotes to Overcome Fear
& Ultimately Earn Millions at www.177Quotes.com

Affirmation #60

I am free of fear, doubt, procrastination
and low self-belief NOW!

Affirmation #61

I am only associating with encouraging,
empowering, enthusiastic Champions.

Affirmation #62

Listen up and listen good – Fear be gone
NOW out of my life!

Affirmation #63

I am an action taking, fear demolishing,
eye opening, mind blowing, laser focused
Champion.

Grab a Hold of John's FREE Video...   17
The Top *11* Motivational Quotes to Overcome Fear
& Ultimately Earn Millions at www.177Quotes.com

Affirmation #64

I am activating Prosperity in
my life NOW!

Affirmation #65

Never again will I retreat when the
enemy of fear attacks my dream.

Affirmation #66

I am controlling my future with
every word.

Affirmation #67

I am slaying debt out of my life!

Grab a Hold of John's FREE Video...   18
The Top *11* Motivational Quotes to Overcome Fear
& Ultimately Earn Millions at www.177Quotes.com

Affirmation #68

I am overcoming the lack mentality by developing my Champion faith muscle.

Affirmation #69

I am living in an organized, forward moving, profitable, life-changing, construction zone.

Affirmation #70

My daily decisions determine my ultimate destiny.

Affirmation #71

I have the right to earn a huge income.

Grab a Hold of John's FREE Video...　　19
The Top *11* Motivational Quotes to Overcome Fear
& Ultimately Earn Millions at www.177Quotes.com

Affirmation #72

I am a faith building, no holds barred,
Why Warrior Champion.

Affirmation #73

I am a persistent, patient, palm tree root
building, overcoming Champion.

Affirmation #74

I am commanding a miracle in my life!

Affirmation #75

I am receiving only the truth about
myself. I refuse to listen to naysayers!

Grab a Hold of John's FREE Video... 20
The Top *11* Motivational Quotes to Overcome Fear
& Ultimately Earn Millions at www.177Quotes.com

Affirmation #76

I am the Commander and Chief of my Why.

Affirmation #77

Hey fear...I am demanding that you turn around and get out of my life now!

Affirmation #78

I am activating my faith with my faith-filled, fear destroying, belief building words

Affirmation #79

I am taking advantage of pressure to refine my dream now.

Grab a Hold of John's FREE Video... 21
The Top *11* Motivational Quotes to Overcome Fear
& Ultimately Earn Millions at www.177Quotes.com

Affirmation #80

Pressure empowers me to soar
like an eagle.

Affirmation #81

It's an unanimous decision...I am a laser
focused Champion that will achieve
my Why!

Affirmation #82

My dream is my dream and I am
responsible for it.

Affirmation #83

My future is crystal clear and full of
miracles.

Grab a Hold of John's FREE Video...   22
The Top *11* Motivational Quotes to Overcome Fear
& Ultimately Earn Millions at www.177Quotes.com

Affirmation #84

I am rolling over each morning and expecting supernatural miracles.

Affirmation #85

I am willing to faithfully fight for my Why in life.

Affirmation #86

I am an Achiever!

Affirmation #87

I am releasing the shackles to my past right now!

Grab a Hold of John's FREE Video... 23
The Top *11* Motivational Quotes to Overcome Fear
& Ultimately Earn Millions at www.177Quotes.com

Affirmation #88

I am catapulting my success now!

Affirmation #89

I am walking with the armor of faith around me every day as I build my Why.

Affirmation #90

I am bombarding myself with self-belief to destroy the internal lying words of fear.

Affirmation #91

Bring it on! I am prepared to defeat the enemy that is stealing my dreams.

Grab a Hold of John's FREE Video...   24
The Top *11* Motivational Quotes to Overcome Fear
& Ultimately Earn Millions at www.177Quotes.com

Affirmation #92

I am consistently and constantly building my belief structure with my Why Rollover in the mornings.

Affirmation #93

I am a fear demolisher!

Affirmation #94

My habits guarantee miracles!

Affirmation #95

I am digging down deep, building the Champion root structure to withstand the enemy's attack.

Grab a Hold of John's FREE Video... 25
The Top *11* Motivational Quotes to Overcome Fear
& Ultimately Earn Millions at www.177Quotes.com

Affirmation #96

I am phenomenally successful.

Affirmation #97

I am a finisher!

Affirmation #98

I am declaring and decreeing miracles in my life now!

Affirmation #99

I am a joyous giver!

Affirmation #100

I am relentlessly pursuing my dream!

Grab a Hold of John's FREE Video...   26
The Top *11* Motivational Quotes to Overcome Fear
& Ultimately Earn Millions at www.177Quotes.com

Affirmation #101

I am solely guided by achieving my Why.

Affirmation #102

I am wired for warfare to combat
the enemy of fear and procrastination.

Affirmation #103

I am a Why Warrior Champion that
will win!

Affirmation #104

I am listening to my dream daily!

Grab a Hold of John's FREE Video... 27
The Top *11* Motivational Quotes to Overcome Fear
& Ultimately Earn Millions at www.177Quotes.com

Affirmation #105

I am confident in my abilities!

Affirmation #106

I am faithfully resting in my belief to achieve my Why.

Affirmation #107

I am relentlessly speaking my Why into existence.

Affirmation #108

I am eliminating ALL distractions now in my live to ultimately live my Why.

Grab a Hold of John's FREE Video...   28
The Top *11* Motivational Quotes to Overcome Fear
& Ultimately Earn Millions at www.177Quotes.com

Affirmation #109

I am overflowing with faithful enthusiasm!

Affirmation #110

I am releasing a supernatural harvest today with my actions and words.

Affirmation #111

My belief is rock-solid and bulletproof.

Affirmation #112

I am a Champion Decision Maker!

Grab a Hold of John's FREE Video... 29
The Top *11* Motivational Quotes to Overcome Fear
& Ultimately Earn Millions at www.177Quotes.com

Affirmation #113

My faith foundation is growing deeper
and higher every day.

Affirmation #114

I am predicting my miracle harvest with
my Champion schedule.

Affirmation #115

I am changing lives by closing
business today!

Affirmation #116

I am worthy of monumental success!
Yes ME!

Grab a Hold of John's FREE Video...   30
The Top *11* Motivational Quotes to Overcome Fear
& Ultimately Earn Millions at www.177Quotes.com

Affirmation #117

My schedule will predict my results.

Affirmation #118

I am persistently patient to press on to achieve my Why NOW!

Affirmation #119

I am free of excuses!

Affirmation #120

I am ready for a Champion breakthrough!

Grab a Hold of John's FREE Video...   31
The Top *11* Motivational Quotes to Overcome Fear
& Ultimately Earn Millions at www.177Quotes.com

Affirmation #121

My habits predict supernatural miracles.

Affirmation #122

I am earning huge income, because I am focused on making a difference in the world.

Affirmation #123

I am highly motivated to achieve my dreams!

Affirmation #124

I am totally immersed in proven, time-tested personal development every day.

Grab a Hold of John's FREE Video... 32
The Top *11* Motivational Quotes to Overcome Fear
& Ultimately Earn Millions at www.177Quotes.com

Affirmation #125

I am speaking power-packed, dynamic energizing words.

Affirmation #126

I am speaking words of increase 24 hours a day 7 days a week.

Affirmation #127

I am exercising daily to live the healthiest lifestyle possible.

Affirmation #128

I am challenging myself second by second to be the best that I can be.

Grab a Hold of John's FREE Video... 33
The Top *11* Motivational Quotes to Overcome Fear
& Ultimately Earn Millions at www.177Quotes.com

Affirmation #129

My words are explosive!

Affirmation #130

I am a certified winner by birthright!

Affirmation #131

I am a creative, life-changing, miracle manifesting Why Warrior.

Affirmation #132

I am believing in miracles now for me!

Affirmation #133

I am receiving my miracle today!

Grab a Hold of John's FREE Video... 34
The Top *11* Motivational Quotes to Overcome Fear
& Ultimately Earn Millions at www.177Quotes.com

Affirmation #134

I am living a remarkable, wonderful,
breathtaking, amazing, joyful life!

Affirmation #135

I am challenging myself each day to get
to the next level, because I have
the right to.

Affirmation #136

I am free of fear, doubt, procrastination,
and low self-belief NOW!

Affirmation #137

My mastermind team consists exclusively
of empowering Champions!

Grab a Hold of John's FREE Video...   35
The Top *11* Motivational Quotes to Overcome Fear
& Ultimately Earn Millions at www.177Quotes.com

Affirmation #138

My mastermind is full of honor and
integrity that love me and my dream

Affirmation #139

I am deleting ALL negative naysayers out
of my life NOW!

Affirmation #140

I am a Champion preparing for record-
breaking victories.

Affirmation #141

I will not retreat when the enemy tries
to defeat my dream – bring it on!

Grab a Hold of John's FREE Video...   36
The Top *11* Motivational Quotes to Overcome Fear
& Ultimately Earn Millions at www.177Quotes.com

Affirmation #142

My uncomfortable, challenging daily actions predict my miracle results.

Affirmation #143

I am a Champion butterfly!

Affirmation #144

I am living a healthy lifestyle!

Affirmation #145

I am forever thankful for all of my blessings in life.

Grab a Hold of John's FREE Video...   37
The Top *11* Motivational Quotes to Overcome Fear
& Ultimately Earn Millions at www.177Quotes.com

Affirmation #146

I choose to win!

Affirmation #147

I am accepting my challenges each day
to explode out of my comfort zone.

Affirmation #148

I am committed to eliminating all
negativity out of my life.

Affirmation #149

I am empowered to prosper by my
birthright.

Grab a Hold of John's FREE Video... 38
The Top *11* Motivational Quotes to Overcome Fear
& Ultimately Earn Millions at www.177Quotes.com

Affirmation #150

I am an energetic closer!

Affirmation #151

I am a beautiful butterfly struggling to
free myself from my cocoon.

Affirmation #152

I am making miracles out of my
past mistakes.

Affirmation #153

I am stepping over the fear line into faith
land today.

Grab a Hold of John's FREE Video...   39
The Top *11* Motivational Quotes to Overcome Fear
& Ultimately Earn Millions at www.177Quotes.com

Affirmation #154

I am building my testimonial today by speaking words of faith over my life.

Affirmation #155

I am learning to lose my ego!

Affirmation #156

Fear will not stop me from achieving my Why in life.

Affirmation #157

I am a generous and joyful giver!

Grab a Hold of John's FREE Video... 40
The Top *11* Motivational Quotes to Overcome Fear
& Ultimately Earn Millions at www.177Quotes.com

Affirmation #158

I live to give!

Affirmation #159

My harvest is coming, because I have planted seeds of greatness.

Affirmation #160

I am listening to my mentor today with open ears, eyes, heart and mind.

Affirmation #161

I am releasing the stubbornness spirit in order to grow.

Grab a Hold of John's FREE Video... 41
The Top *11* Motivational Quotes to Overcome Fear
& Ultimately Earn Millions at www.177Quotes.com

Affirmation #162

I am highly blessed and positioned for
supernatural increase.

Affirmation #163

I am shocking my bank teller as I deposit
my harvest check.

Affirmation #164

I am building my dream 1000%
on a daily basis.

Affirmation #165

I am decisive about attending live events
to change my life.

Grab a Hold of John's FREE Video... 42
The Top *11* Motivational Quotes to Overcome Fear
& Ultimately Earn Millions at www.177Quotes.com

Affirmation #166

I believe that I will achieve my Why!

Affirmation #167

I am associating with ONLY laser focused, dream building, fired up, Why Warrior Champions.

Affirmation #168

I am absolutely loving my success struggle.

Affirmation #169

I am fulfilling my God-given destiny!

Grab a Hold of John's FREE Video... 43
The Top *11* Motivational Quotes to Overcome Fear
& Ultimately Earn Millions at www.177Quotes.com

Affirmation #170

I am defeating the enemy mindset
of debt forever!

Affirmation #171

I am listening to the faith in my heart.

Affirmation #172

I am scheduled and detailed in my
daily planning.

Affirmation #173

I am sowing seeds of greatness into the
lives of others.

Grab a Hold of John's FREE Video...   **44**
The Top *11* Motivational Quotes to Overcome Fear
& Ultimately Earn Millions at www.177Quotes.com

Affirmation #174

The impossible is possible for me!

Affirmation #175

I am challenging myself to change my life second by second.

Affirmation #176

I am a leader that empowers others to dream bigger.

Affirmation #177

I am an overcomer and overachiever that is living in the abundant success overflow.

Grab a Hold of John's FREE Video...   45
The Top *11* Motivational Quotes to Overcome Fear
& Ultimately Earn Millions at www.177Quotes.com

Affirmation #178

My Why is the driving force for my consistent, focused daily actions.

Affirmation #179

I am living the Championship life!

Affirmation #180

My success is my responsibility.

Affirmation #181

I refuse to compromise my honor and integrity for anything!

Grab a Hold of John's FREE Video... 46
The Top *11* Motivational Quotes to Overcome Fear
& Ultimately Earn Millions at www.177Quotes.com

Affirmation #182

There are no cracks in my cement foundation of faith.

Affirmation #183

Storms in life make me stronger and more confident in my Why Warrior journey.

Affirmation #184

I respect my time and refuse to waste it.

Affirmation #185

I am on a mission to manifest my miracle!

Grab a Hold of John's FREE Video...   47
The Top *11* Motivational Quotes to Overcome Fear
& Ultimately Earn Millions at www.177Quotes.com

Affirmation #186

I am opening long-term, profitable, life-changing relationships.

Affirmation #187

I am confident, because I dress for success and deserve to achieve my Why!

Affirmation #188

Preparation predicts my prosperity!

Affirmation #189

I am the light in the darkness.

Grab a Hold of John's FREE Video... 48
The Top *11* Motivational Quotes to Overcome Fear
& Ultimately Earn Millions at www.177Quotes.com

Affirmation #190

I am destined to change my life NOW!

Affirmation #191

I am achieving Lifestyle Freedom!

Affirmation #192

My schedule represents my results.

Affirmation #193

I honor my Why and my Word daily.

Affirmation #194

I do what I say I am going to do plus I
follow through 1000%.

Grab a Hold of John's FREE Video... 49
The Top *11* Motivational Quotes to Overcome Fear
& Ultimately Earn Millions at www.177Quotes.com

Affirmation #195

I have a responsibility to change lives.

Affirmation #196

I am increasing my dream building every day to build my belief.

Affirmation #197

I am earning more by learning more!

Affirmation #198

I am achieving new results simply because my new actions guarantee it.

Grab a Hold of John's FREE Video...   50
The Top *11* Motivational Quotes to Overcome Fear
& Ultimately Earn Millions at www.177Quotes.com

Affirmation #199

I am annihilating the enemies of fear, doubt and procrastination out of my life!

Affirmation #200

I am a Why Warrior ready to fight for my dream.

Affirmation #201

I am accountable for my daily actions.

Affirmation #202

My mastermind team moves me to a higher level.

Grab a Hold of John's FREE Video...   51
The Top *11* Motivational Quotes to Overcome Fear
& Ultimately Earn Millions at www.177Quotes.com

Affirmation #203

I am washing my brain daily with positive motivation.

Affirmation #204

I am an outstanding steward of my money.

Affirmation #205

I have an attitude of gratitude!

Affirmation #206

I sow my seeds into good soil.

Grab a Hold of John's FREE Video... 52
The Top *11* Motivational Quotes to Overcome Fear
& Ultimately Earn Millions at www.177Quotes.com

Affirmation #207

I REFUSE to quit!

Affirmation #208

My mouth will make me a Millionaire!

Affirmation #209

I am blessed beyond measure.

Affirmation #210

Champions live free, and I am a Free
Champion Now!

Grab a Hold of John's FREE Video... 53
The Top *11* Motivational Quotes to Overcome Fear
& Ultimately Earn Millions at www.177Quotes.com

Affirmation #211

I am absolutely determined to demolish fear daily.

Affirmation #212

I am actively listening to dream BIG!

Affirmation #213

I am destroying doubt with my outwardly spoken faith-filled words.

Affirmation #214

Today is my day for a breakthrough!

Grab a Hold of John's FREE Video... 54
The Top *11* Motivational Quotes to Overcome Fear
& Ultimately Earn Millions at www.177Quotes.com

Affirmation #215

I am the CEO of my Billion Dollar Company!

Affirmation #216

I am the owner of my dream not you!

Affirmation #217

I am in a record-breaking season.

Affirmation #218

I am worthy of receiving my dream!

Affirmation #219

No matter what...I WIN!

Grab a Hold of John's FREE Video... 55
The Top *11* Motivational Quotes to Overcome Fear
& Ultimately Earn Millions at www.177Quotes.com

Affirmation #220

I am a tenaciously passionate, committed, unshakable Why Warrior!

Affirmation #221

That's right fear...Access DENIED Forever!

Affirmation #222

I am a rock-solid, honorable, born winner making a difference.

Affirmation #223

I am 1000% emotionally connected to my Why. Get out of my way fear!

Grab a Hold of John's FREE Video... 56
The Top *11* Motivational Quotes to Overcome Fear
& Ultimately Earn Millions at www.177Quotes.com

Affirmation #224

You better not challenge my commitment or else you'll feel the power of a Why Warrior Champion!

Affirmation #225

Right now, I am better than ever because of my focused preparation.

Affirmation #226

I am an income generating, donation giving, Millionaire machine!

Affirmation #227

Faith is my fuel, and I am a Why Warrior fighter jet.

Grab a Hold of John's FREE Video... 57
The Top *11* Motivational Quotes to Overcome Fear
& Ultimately Earn Millions at www.177Quotes.com

Affirmation #228

Pay Attention! It is official...you have been deleted out of my life forever!

Affirmation #229

By my birthright, I have earned the right to change lives.

Affirmation #230

I am a record-breaking, supernaturally blessed Why Warrior!

Affirmation #231

I am standing strong in the face of adversity to strengthen my foundation.

Grab a Hold of John's FREE Video...   58
The Top *11* Motivational Quotes to Overcome Fear
& Ultimately Earn Millions at www.177Quotes.com

Affirmation #232

I am a Champion Habit Maker!

Affirmation #233

That's right! I am believing in jaw-dropping miracles for me.

Affirmation #234

Watch out supernatural miracle...here I come to own you!

Affirmation #235

Determination is my middle name!

Grab a Hold of John's FREE Video... 59
The Top *11* Motivational Quotes to Overcome Fear
& Ultimately Earn Millions at www.177Quotes.com

Affirmation #236

I am a lifetime Why Warrior committed
to miracle achievement.

Affirmation #237

I am on high alert 24 hours a day for the
deadly dream destroying fear flu.

Affirmation #238

I am an eyeball popping, jaw dropping,
bank teller shocking, million dollar giving
Why Warrior Champion!

Affirmation #239

I am determined to protect myself from
the enemy every second of every day!

Grab a Hold of John's FREE Video...   60
The Top *11* Motivational Quotes to Overcome Fear
& Ultimately Earn Millions at www.177Quotes.com

Affirmation #240

I am a believing, motivating, life-changing, procrastination conquering Champion!

Affirmation #241

I am a faithful, fear destroying, motivated Millionaire!

Affirmation #242

My code name is Commitment!

Affirmation #243

All things are possible with my Why Warrior *7* minute morning rollover.

Grab a Hold of John's FREE Video... 61
The Top *11* Motivational Quotes to Overcome Fear
& Ultimately Earn Millions at www.177Quotes.com

Affirmation #244

Excuse me! Who are you? Get out of my way default!

Affirmation #245

I am dedicated to the achievement of my Why in life 1000%.

Affirmation #246

I am the master over my daily decisions to break records.

Affirmation #247

I am fired up and laser-focused! I do not multi-task or tolerate distractions.

Grab a Hold of John's FREE Video...   62
The Top *11* Motivational Quotes to Overcome Fear
& Ultimately Earn Millions at www.177Quotes.com

Affirmation #248

I am energetically, aggressively, flawlessly achieving my miracle in life.

Affirmation #249

I am an important part of changing the world! Yes ME!

Affirmation #250

I am an outward expression of inward laser-focused Champion habits.

Affirmation #251

I am led by my Why!

Grab a Hold of John's FREE Video... 63
The Top *11* Motivational Quotes to Overcome Fear
& Ultimately Earn Millions at www.177Quotes.com

Affirmation #252

Preparation and dedication are what my actions represent daily.

Affirmation #253

Failure and quitting are not options as long as I am in my Why Warrior Success journey.

Affirmation #254

Abundance is overflowing in every area of my life!

Affirmation #255

I choose to stand on the *5* year faithful Why Warrior plan of action.

Grab a Hold of John's FREE Video...   64
The Top *11* Motivational Quotes to Overcome Fear
& Ultimately Earn Millions at www.177Quotes.com

Affirmation #256

I am defying the odds to break records
and shock my bank teller!

Affirmation #257

I am speaking victories into existence
right now in my life!

Affirmation #258

I am walking in the highly-guarded, fully
protected, Why Warrior miracle zone.

Affirmation #259

I am attacking my weakness with all out
faith in myself as a Why Warrior
Champion!

Grab a Hold of John's FREE Video... 65
The Top *11* Motivational Quotes to Overcome Fear
& Ultimately Earn Millions at www.177Quotes.com

Affirmation #260

I am a strategic, record-breaking Champion willing do every day what others only think about doing occasionally.

Affirmation #261

I am taking back what fear tried to take away from me right NOW!

Affirmation #262

I am consistently keeping the miracle winning edge in my life.

Affirmation #263

How sweet it is to live my life laser-focused and fired up every single day.

Grab a Hold of John's FREE Video...   66
The Top *11* Motivational Quotes to Overcome Fear
& Ultimately Earn Millions at www.177Quotes.com

Affirmation #264

I am sharpening my Why Warrior motivational marketing edge by listening to challenging, truthful wisdom.

Affirmation #265

I am deleting ALL whiners out of my life Now!

Affirmation #266

I am a responsible Champion dedicated to living life to the fullest.

Affirmation #267

I am known worldwide as a dreamer that achieved my Why!

Grab a Hold of John's FREE Video... 67
The Top *11* Motivational Quotes to Overcome Fear
& Ultimately Earn Millions at www.177Quotes.com

Affirmation #268

I am willing to pay the price and go the extra mile because I am worthy of living my dream!

Affirmation #269

Fear will never be able to defeat a laser-focused Why Warrior Champion!

Affirmation #270

My fuel is my dream and my fuel tank is overflowing with faith.

Affirmation #271

I am an extreme dreamer motivated to achieve my jaw-dropping dreams!

Grab a Hold of John's FREE Video...   68
The Top *11* Motivational Quotes to Overcome Fear
& Ultimately Earn Millions at www.177Quotes.com

Affirmation #272

Lifestyle Freedom is my birthright, and fear will never stop me from having it ever again!

Affirmation #273

My Why can trust me 1000% to stay committed for the rest of my life.

Affirmation #274

Each and every day, I am discovering deep down exactly who I want to be, and the possibilities are endless.

Affirmation #275

I am planning second by second for the guaranteed achievement of my Why.

Grab a Hold of John's FREE Video... 69
The Top *11* Motivational Quotes to Overcome Fear
& Ultimately Earn Millions at www.177Quotes.com

Affirmation #276

I am a Champion showing others how to live the Champion life by my outwardly spoken words and honorable actions.

Affirmation #277

I am a living, breathing, shining example of what daily focused, uncomfortable action can accomplish.

Affirmation #278

I am a dream building machine!

Affirmation #279

I believe in the miraculous supernatural process of changing my life!

Grab a Hold of John's FREE Video...   70
The Top *11* Motivational Quotes to Overcome Fear
& Ultimately Earn Millions at www.177Quotes.com

Affirmation #280

I am building a life-long strategic plan of action to accomplish my mission.

Affirmation #281

I believe in my incorruptible, determined dream inside of me!

Affirmation #282

My Why Warrior success road is paved with opportunity and endless possibilities.

Affirmation #283

I am conquering my fears to achieve my dreams!

Grab a Hold of John's FREE Video... 71
The Top *11* Motivational Quotes to Overcome Fear
& Ultimately Earn Millions at www.177Quotes.com

Affirmation #284

The enemy wants to stop me, but I will never quit on me or my Why! Get out of my way NOW enemy!

Affirmation #285

I have the right to live my dreams and be free! I will no longer let society determine my level of success.

Affirmation #286

I am leaving a long-lasting legacy for my family!

Affirmation #287

My Why is more than enough for me to press on through any adversity and win!

Grab a Hold of John's FREE Video... 72
The Top *11* Motivational Quotes to Overcome Fear
& Ultimately Earn Millions at www.177Quotes.com

Affirmation #288

I live by faith built on the belief that I was born a Champion.

Affirmation #289

I chose success over failure...no more whining about how hard it is to achieve!

Affirmation #290

My Why keeps me nourished to prosper through the rainy season.

Affirmation #291

I can and will change the world through my honor, integrity and commitment.

Grab a Hold of John's FREE Video...   73
The Top *11* Motivational Quotes to Overcome Fear
& Ultimately Earn Millions at www.177Quotes.com

Affirmation #292

I will rise to the occasion every time that my dream calls me to step out in faith!

Affirmation #293

I am shouting my Why out loud in the face of the enemy every day.

Affirmation #294

Today is the day that abundant overflow happens in my life.

Affirmation #295

Have you heard the news? I won the fear versus faith battle!

Grab a Hold of John's FREE Video... 74
The Top *11* Motivational Quotes to Overcome Fear
& Ultimately Earn Millions at www.177Quotes.com

Affirmation #296

I am walking strong in the atmosphere of confidence as I achieve my Why!

Affirmation #297

The cycle of defeat has stopped as of right now! I am defending my birthright to live a Champion life!

Affirmation #298

I am rock-solid in my daily determination to listen, apply and implement proven Why Warrior strategies.

Affirmation #299

I don't drink the WHINE juice! Excuses have no place in my life anymore!

Grab a Hold of John's FREE Video... 75
The Top *11* Motivational Quotes to Overcome Fear
& Ultimately Earn Millions at www.177Quotes.com

Affirmation #300

Unless you speak faith-filled words, I will tune you out! I only listen to the Why Warrior success channel.

Affirmation #301

I possess undeniable courage to stand up for my God-given right to live a life of integrity. I will not compromise!

Affirmation #302

I am living all out every day expecting my Miracle!

Affirmation #303

I accept challenges to develop my bulletproof cement commitment!

Grab a Hold of John's FREE Video... 76
The Top *11* Motivational Quotes to Overcome Fear
& Ultimately Earn Millions at www.177Quotes.com

Affirmation #304

My results are my responsibility!

Affirmation #305

My decisions are based in faithful expectation.

Affirmation #306

Shhh...I am listening to my Why!

Affirmation #307

I am certified by my Champion birth certificate to live a life of abundant overflow and bountiful blessings.

Grab a Hold of John's FREE Video... 77
The Top *11* Motivational Quotes to Overcome Fear
& Ultimately Earn Millions at www.177Quotes.com

Affirmation #308

Nothing in this world has the guaranteed mountain moving power of my words.

Affirmation #309

I am personally prepared to make decisions that will ultimately lead to living lifestyle freedom forever.

Affirmation #310

I am absolutely committed for as long as it takes no matter what it takes to achieve my Why.

Affirmation #311

I love my Why, and my Why loves me!

Grab a Hold of John's FREE Video...   78
The Top *11* Motivational Quotes to Overcome Fear
& Ultimately Earn Millions at www.177Quotes.com

Affirmation #312

I am not interested in hearing
your excuses!

Affirmation #313

I am raising the bar of my commitment
so high that excuses can't jump up and
pull me down.

Affirmation #314

Victory is mine now! I am a victorious
Eagle Champion!

Affirmation #315

I am willing to risk it all for my Why!

Grab a Hold of John's FREE Video...   79
The Top *11* Motivational Quotes to Overcome Fear
& Ultimately Earn Millions at www.177Quotes.com

Affirmation #316

I am a conqueror in all areas of my Why
Warrior Champion life!

Affirmation #317

I am standing strong on cement
commitment and keeping fear out of my
life forever!

Affirmation #318

I am giving away more than I am
keeping! I am a Champion giver!

Affirmation #319

I will withstand all the attacks by fear to
destroy my Why! I am a fighter!

Grab a Hold of John's FREE Video...   80
The Top *11* Motivational Quotes to Overcome Fear
& Ultimately Earn Millions at www.177Quotes.com

Affirmation #320

When everyone else quits, I will stand strong for my Why!

Affirmation #321

My success attitude is driven by my belief in my Why.

Affirmation #322

My environment smells like a miracle!

Affirmation #323

Can't you see that I have my DO NOT DISTURB ears on and you are in my Millionaire Champion Zone!

Grab a Hold of John's FREE Video... 81
The Top *11* Motivational Quotes to Overcome Fear
& Ultimately Earn Millions at www.177Quotes.com

Affirmation #324

I am increasing my Dream Fuel daily with my morning preparation.

Affirmation #325

I live and breathe in an atmosphere of expectation that I will achieve my Why!

Affirmation #326

I am turning past mistakes into future miracles!

Affirmation #327

I am a strategic, systematic Why Warrior planning and preparing for my miracle!

Grab a Hold of John's FREE Video...   82
The Top *11* Motivational Quotes to Overcome Fear
& Ultimately Earn Millions at www.177Quotes.com

Affirmation #328

I am consistently deleting the negative
fear flu out of my life!

Affirmation #329

I respond to the call of my Why by taking
uncomfortable, challenging action.

Affirmation #330

I am persevering no matter what anyone
else does around me!

Affirmation #331

My Why Warrior status is obvious to
others because of my belief in myself
and my Why in life.

Grab a Hold of John's FREE Video... 83
The Top *11* Motivational Quotes to Overcome Fear
& Ultimately Earn Millions at www.177Quotes.com

Affirmation #332

I am prepared to handle anything when fear tries to knock me down!

Affirmation #333

I am determined to achieve my Why no matter what comes my way.

Affirmation #334

Never again will I question my God-given dream!

Affirmation #335

I am dedicated to being laser-focused every second of my day.

Grab a Hold of John's FREE Video... 84
The Top *11* Motivational Quotes to Overcome Fear
& Ultimately Earn Millions at www.177Quotes.com

Affirmation #336

Every one of my words are worth millions!

Affirmation #337

I am gradually achieving my goals one by one despite the obstacles that I face.

Affirmation #338

I am laser-focused to conquer fear!

Affirmation #339

My confidence is an immovable brick wall that the enemy will never penetrate.

Grab a Hold of John's FREE Video...   85
The Top *11* Motivational Quotes to Overcome Fear
& Ultimately Earn Millions at www.177Quotes.com

Affirmation #340

I am a worldwide inspiration proving that when a decision is made nothing can stop you from achieving your dreams!

Affirmation #341

The relentless pursuit of my Why will lead to its achievement.

Affirmation #342

Nothing will ever again detour me off my Why Warrior Success Journey.

Affirmation #343

My heart cries out with the emotions that my Why is seeking from me.

Grab a Hold of John's FREE Video...   86
The Top *11* Motivational Quotes to Overcome Fear
& Ultimately Earn Millions at www.177Quotes.com

Affirmation #344

My Why leads me in the right direction, and I will continue to follow its path.

Affirmation #345

I am a respecter of my dreams by my daily action steps.

Affirmation #346

I am a Champion no matter what anyone else says. I believe in ME!

Affirmation #347

I am challenging deadly indecision with my decisive Why Warrior actions.

Grab a Hold of John's FREE Video...   87
The Top *11* Motivational Quotes to Overcome Fear
& Ultimately Earn Millions at www.177Quotes.com

Affirmation #348

I am finding my Why more and more because of my consistent self-development daily habits.

Affirmation #349

I have the authority to not listen to you if you are a dream stealer!

Affirmation #350

I am soaring higher and higher to find my Why!

Affirmation #351

Today is the day that my miracle explodes through and proves everyone wrong about me and my Why!

Grab a Hold of John's FREE Video... 88
The Top *11* Motivational Quotes to Overcome Fear
& Ultimately Earn Millions at www.177Quotes.com

Affirmation #352

I am an overcomer of obstacles!

Affirmation #353

My Why is just warming up! Watch out, because there is so much more to come!

Affirmation #354

I am equipped with 1000% conviction that I was born a Champion!

Affirmation #355

I am actively engaged in guarding my eyes and ears from negative influences of the world that will only destroy my dreams and goals!

Grab a Hold of John's FREE Video... 89
The Top *11* Motivational Quotes to Overcome Fear
& Ultimately Earn Millions at www.177Quotes.com

Affirmation #356

I am a trustworthy Why Warrior!

Affirmation #357

I am a faith fighting, enemy defeating
Why Warrior Champion!

Affirmation #358

People are asking me every day...How did
you do it?

Affirmation #359

I am willing to listen to my heart and
trust it enough to step out in faith.

Grab a Hold of John's FREE Video... 90
The Top *11* Motivational Quotes to Overcome Fear
& Ultimately Earn Millions at www.177Quotes.com

Affirmation #360

I am fully embracing my future miracle!

Affirmation #361

I am dressing for supernatural success inside and out every day.

Affirmation #362

I am extremely dedicated to making a difference in lives around the world!

Affirmation #363

I am celebrating the gift of life that I have every single day!

Grab a Hold of John's FREE Video...   91
The Top *11* Motivational Quotes to Overcome Fear
& Ultimately Earn Millions at www.177Quotes.com

Affirmation #364

My heart holds the key to my dreams and the achievement of my Why.

Affirmation #365

I am committed to do whatever it takes for as long as it takes to be a Why Warrior 1000%!